"The Echoes of the Timber Wolf"
A Study in the Life of King David

The Echoes of the Timber Wolf: A Study in the Life of King David

Trilogy Christian Publishers A Wholly Owned Subsidiary of Trinity Broadcasting Network

2442 Michelle Drive Tustin, CA 92780

Rights Department, 2442 Michelle Drive, Tustin, CA 92780.

Trilogy Christian Publishing/TBN and colophon are trademarks of Trinity Broadcasting Network.

For information about special discounts for bulk purchases, please contact Trilogy Christian Publishing.

Trilogy Disclaimer: The views and content expressed in this book are those of the author and may not necessarily reflect the views and doctrine of Trilogy Christian Publishing or the Trinity Broadcasting Network.

Manufactured in the United States of America

10 9 8 7 6 5 4 3 2 1

Library of Congress Cataloging-in-Publication Data is available.

ISBN: 978-1-63769-692-7

E-ISBN: 978-1-63769-693-4

Dedication

This book is dedicated to Rev. Dr. Mark T. Oliver of Trinity Baptist Church of Brockton, Massachusett, of whom I was discipled into pastoral ministry . And Rev. Mike Rivera and Rev. Baron Rodrigues who charged me before Christ's holy angels into the pastoral ministry.

"So Jesse sent for him. He was dark and handsome, with beautiful eyes. And the Lord said, 'This is the one; anoint him.' So as David stood there among his brothers, Samuel took the flask of olive oil he had brought and anointed David with the oil. And the Spirit of the Lord came powerfully upon David from that day on. Then Samuel returned to Ramah" (1 Samuel 16:12-13).

Acknowledgements

I'd like to thank all the staff at Trilogy Publishing for their help and support in helping me to create and publish my dream book. And to all the authors over the years who have written about David and provided vast knowledge on the subject of David to whom my education on David I owe much credit to.

Table of Contents

Prologue

Have you ever sought the courage to face life's trials? Have you ever felt like you were too far away from God because the distress of life was hindering your blessings? Journey with me to hear the echoes of the timber wolf and hear the voice that encouraged David to be a mighty warrior, and King. Learn how the anointing of Samuel gave David the staying power he needed, how King Saul's relentless pursuit of him made him who he became: the legendary King of Israel. The scene is old Palestine. Among the poor of the people, a nation with grand history, and the creator of the world as their God. The issue at hand is the desire and need for a King. And the answer is God's selection of David as King.

Preface

The Echoes of the Timber Wolf came into being when I was homeless, and God used the appearance of a wolf to encourage me and bring me to new heights of spirituality. I wrote this book because I've always been fascinated with David. Since I've read so much about him over the years, I decided I would write some of my own thoughts of him, seeing that he is such an important person, in history and in the biblical text. My hope is that you would enjoy learning about such a legendary man and servant of God.

Foreword

I have known Jean Belizaire for 17 years. We have served in church ministry together. From the time I met him, it was clear that Jean's main desire was to help others learn about the forgiveness of God in Jesus Christ, as well as the deep truths of God's desire for each person. This study in the life of King David is only an extension of that desire. The author reminds us that "David was made strong through his troubles".

We all have troubles that must be navigated from which we must learn about God and ourselves. This is why David is so fascinating to many of us. We each can identify with his failures as well as his struggles, and Jean is no exception. Many of his insights in this book come from his own struggles.

As Jean learns from his study of life with the life and heart of David as a guide , he now turns and shares it with us. In the end, David grows through his weakness. And in prayer, finds courage to put God first. He finds his way to be "more concerned about the fame of God." May we all, through our own failures and troubles, find our way to that same heart.

Mark T. Oliver

Trinity Baptist Church

Senior Pastor

Introduction

King David's story is a story that legends are made of, from his journey as a poor shepherd's boy tending the sheep in the blazing heat of Palestine land and to his defeat of a Nephilim hybrid of a man that stood nine feet and nine inches tall named "Goliath of Gath," to gaining the confidence of his people being a representative of the poor and disinherited,to being hounded in a massive manhunt by a jealous and delusional king.

To the treachery of adultery and a murder to cover up his sins, to being a man after Gods own heart, and to a curse that would never leave his home. David is the most complex and incongruous man in the pages of the Bible yet: still beloved of God. Come and journey with me into the life of King David where we shall discover why his soul was loved by God, and we shall hear the echoes of the timber wolf in his story.

Chapter 1
God's Echo Cardiogram

The echo cardiogram is a test that does an ultra-sound test of the Heart. It hears the sound and it seeks to see if there is any existing problem or underlying heart condition. It surfaces the heart beat to discover its strength or its weakness, and in the story of David we discover that his heart is at the center of discussion when being anointed and selected as king of Israel.

....

In comparison to David, Israel's first king was disobedient, prideful, and reckless. It seems as if God, from the beginning of his reign, was not disposed that he should be a king because the idea of a monarch was of the people and not of God. Prophecies went forward warning the people of what their elected monarch would do.

Saul's heart was weak from the onset hiding "amongst the stuff" he was tall and handsome but not of the courage of David.

Saul disqualified himself because his heart was not right for the position. Pride was the underlying heart condition of his internal self. And his disobedience would prove to be the end of his position and reign. He would later lose control of himself and become a madman bent on revenge of a young man who would have the praises of the people.

David on the other hand was in the clay hills of Palestine, doing menial work, watching the herds of sheep and goats. But David is found by God, he is called a king before ever being crowned one, a warrior before ever having a fight, judicious and wise before ever having a critical decision to make, handsome featured before having the love of women, and gifted before ever recording a Psalm...

Gods echo cardiogram tests the heart, for the heart is the center of one's being, especially in matters of prominence. One doesn't get promoted until his heart can be seen by God and the people he will serve as strong enough for the job and intentioned about being like God in matters of the people...

The heart is a vital organ in the human body, and metaphorically, and spiritually speaking the heart is essential to one's worship of God. The creator of the universe looks upon the heart, because from there, God can examine one's love for him and one's devotion to him.

With the heart, we are commanded to love God; And with the heart, we relate to Him. No one knows when David began his relationship with God, but when he appears before Goliath in a face-to-face battle, he is zealously taking on the challenge in God's name. His passion to see his name honored was a matter of the heart.

Because God's name is important, it is his character, it is his fame, David was more concerned about the fame of God than Saul. King Saul was concerned about his own personal fame, his own appearance and image, rather than seeing the great Jehovah proclaimed to the ends of the earth! So God could see in the young peasant boy named David that he was concerned about the glories of God, and God would later place glory on him because his heart was for the glory of God!

David did fall short of God's glory, but he never ceased to seek it. His made him a prime candidate to be king, because the Israelites were not seeking his fame in the beginning by asking for a king. It was out of pride that they did, desiring to be like heathen nations around them when Elohim was already their king. However, David came on to the sceene as a man who recognized by the Creator as the true King of the people he had been entrusted with.

In the pages of the Bible, there is a distinct contrast between David and Saul'sinner self. The Holy Spirit did this to show why exactly David came to be a man after God's own heart. The phrase "a man after God's own heart" has been debated hotly over the years amongst theologians and critics alike. It seems as if God is out of place or that the Bible is inaccurate in saying that about David a man who committed the twin sins of adultery and murder, massacred thousands, pridefully numbered Israel, etc.

The thing about God is that He does not measure as we do and seems to stand on a mountain top like a perched eagle with eagle eye vision assessing all things. He knows the soul of a man when it cannot be interpreted by others or by that person himself, because He made the soul and knows what is in a man fully....

King David's heart was sensitive to God. He could hear the voice of God in the midst of the noise of traffic. The still, small voice of God was divine to David. And in turn, made David a righteous man because he cared to heed it. In his soul, he wanted to be in alignment with his creator, whereas Saul was all about his intentions and his will

Saul felt that he was God, that he could do as he pleased, Power does corrupt men, and Saul was corrupted by his own power. We see it in the world today when men in politics get a taste of power and they forget their lowly estate before they had power. They do not realize it is a thing of grace. And such was the case for Saul. And God allowed him to not suffer the consequences of his sin ...

Saul had a great prophet in his life; namely, the Prophet Samuel. He had revelation and guidance. Back then, it was customary for kings to have a prophet both speak to them and guide them in matters pertaining to the throne and war. David had Samuel for a he had died while being a victim of Saul' s mad jealousy.

Later on, King David would have Nathan, a prophet of truth and esteem. God intended a theocratic rule, hence the reason prophets entered palace courts to speak with kings. Saul's heart was never fully repentant, and when he was at a loss for guidance, he consulted the witch of Endor that had a familiar spirit to summon Samuel who had died.

And that in and of itself was forbidden in Israel to practice, but he felt it was okay. In his desperation for guidance and an answer to matters pertaining to the throne, he rationalized it. Desperation can lead to great sin, whereas when David sought God saying things like "Turn and answer me , O lord my God restore the sparkle to my eyes or I will die" (Psalm 13:3).

> "But when David's older brother, Eliab heard David talking to the men, he was angry. 'What are you doing around here anyway?' He demanded, 'What about those few sheep you're supposed to be taking care of? I know about your pride and deceit You just want to see the battle" (1 Samuel 17:28).

Chapter 2

A Misunderstood Blessing

The situation of Goliath demanding a face off with a soldier from the Israelite camp was an intimidating one, because Goliath from Gath was not your average opponent. Some say he was of the generation of the Nephilim, standing 9 feet 9 inches tall, with strength so immense he could carry a 125 pound coat of mail, a spear like a weavers beam , and a helmet of brass upon his head, An armor bearer went before him with a shield, as night and day he intimidated the people....

David appeared on the seen as an errand boy and messenger of his father Jesse, who sent him with a bundle of food for his brothers. Eliab was overwhelmed by the situation but rebuked his brother wrongfully for appearing to think that the battle was fun and games and a means of youthful entertainment for David.

However, he inquired of the situation because he felt he could be of help. Isn't it funny how sometimes we push away people who are potential blessings because we do not understand their motivation or presence in our lives? David's brother had formed an opinion of David that was negative. No one knows when or how it was formed, but nevertheless it was formed and sometimes we need that to be cleared up.

David was a blessing, In the previous chapter, he was anointed by the great prophet Samuel in a secret meeting arranged by God to meet and anoint the new king Eliab was there as a witness to consecration of the new king but seems like his family still didn't think of him that way.

A person can have a great call on their life and people may still not acknowledge it, particularly family and close friends. Thank God our callings are not based on people's approval and their agreement, but it is based on God and his divine beckoning to journey deeper in relationship with Him. Despite one's relationship with others, the journey does not stop because someone feels you should not be on it.

Sometimes life's biggest blessings are misunderstood; so how did this problem get fixed for David? God had to vindicate him from the opinion and attitudes of others. He had to set the record straight so that any misinformation would be ironed out about David, and He did that by giving him an unprecedented victory of Goliath of Gath that would propel David to fame and notoriety.

David's brothers fall out of the story after David's conquest of Goliath.They are not important to the text after that. I can imagine there was some jealousy once Samuel anointed David in the midst of his brothers. As a matter of fact, its interesting that it happened in the midst of them, because David was never publicly acknowledged before that. The truth is, he had the boring task of taking care of sheep, but the heart of a shepherd existed in him.

And that heart, although misunderstood most times, was appreciated by God, and God was making a king out of David when others rejected him. This is where I say be careful how you treat the less fortunate, because God may surprise you by selecting them instead of you and putting them in your face as that special person you rejected and misunderstood.

There are some misunderstandings that happen because communication is not at a good level, or that happen because emotions are high, and we are short circuited by them. But there are some misunderstandings that happen because people have negative thoughts about you. This can only be clarified when people to see your true light and your true self. People need to witness your soul radiating to understand you.

So, David was misunderstood and dealt with contempt from his family. Some even venture to say this was because of his mother and that his mother was a disgraced woman, and hence he was rejected. However, God takes the battered and bruised of life and heals them, send them forth as healing agents, as well minister to the rejected and disinherited.

The Bible says, "Then others began coming - men who were in trouble or in debt or who were just discontented - until David was captain of about 400 men" (1st Samuel 22:2). David became their representative, and to represent the poor and disenfranchised you must be able to understand them. David did because he was like them.

> But David persisted, "I have been taking care of my father's sheep and goats," he said. "When a lion or a bear comes to steal a lamb from the flock, I go after it with a club and rescue the lamb from its mouth. If the animal turns on me, I catch it by the jaw and club it to death. I have done this to both lions and bears, and I'll' do it to this pagan Philistine, too, for he has defied the armies of the living God! The Lord who rescued me from the claws of the lion and the bear will rescue me from this Philistine!" Saul finally consented. "All right, go ahead," he said. "And may the Lord be with you!"(1st Samuel 17:34-37).

Chapter 3

Instinct of an Animal

David had an animal instinct that was sharp and clear. David demonstrated his heart when protecting lambs in his father's flock. His father had given him a charge to keep, a responsibility to uphold, and he did not transgress in this duty of keeping his father's sheep. He loved his charge and the sheep in his care. He could defend them against a hungry and raging lion and ferocious bear.

Instinct is important in leadership; a person has to know how one can be born with animal instinct, but most times it is developed overtime, especially when one is taking on great tasks in the Lord.This makes me think of my former pastor, Mark T.Oliver, who taught me the instincts of a true leader.I didn't realize just how sharp I was until I was launched into pastoral ministry and had to deal with different types of scenarios.It taught me how much instinct was needed and how much I possessed.

If you ever watch animals of the wild, such as a cheetah, they have supreme instinct. Even when they are domesticated and kept in a zoo or as a pet, they never really lose their instinct. If released to the wild they can and will survive because their instinct is inherent.

Inherent instinct knows when something is out of place or wrong. Inherent instinct is the internal discernment factor of the judicious and the pious. Kings possessed it and such was the case with David. When David caught Saul, his enemy, and could've slayed him, he had the gut instinct to leave that up to God, He respected God's sovereignty and respected God's permissive will in letting Saul become king,even though he proved to be a failure at executing God's will.

He also knew that he would be next in line someday. The anointing had taken place, the fatted calf had been sacrificed, God had begun to give him favor with the people. King Saul, was desperate to keep his throne. However, there was a prophecy that it would end. It was only matter of time, and David had the instinct that he would be next All the signs were pointing to this) even Jonathan, Saul's son, had given him some of the clothing off of his back, proving that David indeed was next and not him.

Only asking David to be kind to his house, a thing that David would swear to do ... David had enough wisdom to know that if God wanted to elevate him, that He would in due season and that the spirit of Judgement rested upon Saul because of his disobedient soul. No king could reign in disobedience, and even though David was a marked man because of Saul's jealousy, Saul was marked by God because of his foolish heart to be a deposed king. David was marked by God to be a blessing.

Instinct is that behavior that ensures that a man survives, as it is said, "only the strong survive." It is survival of the fittest" in matters of political challenges and unrest, such in the case of David; and enemies as well.'Some people die off because they cannot survive. They are too weak and fragile of heart to make it. And even Jesus said, "he that endures to the end will be saved."

David was made strong through his troubles. In his reign he would be filled with trouble, and he would have to know God on the level of a survivor and the instincts of a survivor. Survivors have a strength about them, battle scars, and all. I've met addicts who survived horrible life experiences, and even in a weakened state they are still here as a token of Instinct to survive in the wilderness of life.

And David was in the wild most of his life; however, he persisted and was made strong having a survivor's instinct and will.

David put it on, strapped the sword over it, and took a step or two to see what it was like, for he had never worn such things before. "I can't go in these," he protested to Saul. "I'm not used to them." So David took them off again. He picked up five smooth stones from a stream and put them into his shepherd's bag. Then, armed only with his shepherd's staff and sling, he started across the valley to fight the Philistine "(1st Samuel 17:39-40)

Chapter 4

The Art of Spiritual Warfare

Spiritual warfare is real, and you must know how to wage war to win the war. The art of knowing how to wage war can be subjective to how the Lord has trained you. It is true, that the Lord will fight your battles. In other words, if you place your trust in Him. He will deliver you in the midst of the battle. But it is also true that some wars you must fight And you can't always "fight how everyone else fights," because the Lord has trained you otherwise.

David was trained with the lion and the bear when they came to pick the lambs out of the flock of his father. And I believe that God was preparing him for this fight with Goliath. Sometimes, what we go through is preparation for the bigger fights of our lives. We may not understand how winning the major fight will change things for us". If David was defeated by Goliath, he would not have been strategically set up to come to the attention of Saul and people.

He would have had anointing but no reputation; the victory David secured over Goliath secured a reputation for him, and winning with a sling and a stone made it even more glorious. It was indicative of God helping him to fight the battle since David came against Goliath in the name of Yahweh.

Spiritual warfare gives us the grit that we need to serve God in hard Times, Our enemies exist to make us strong. Both physical enemies and spiritual enemies exist to sharpen our senses and make us wise in God. They create a strange power for us over the devil, and bring us to prominence in the spiritual realm.

David was known by the spirits in the spirit realm, because he was to bring Israel and Judah into a strong spiritual state. His leadership would be the means to do so.... (Caveat.. leadership of any kind affects oneself and others spiritually).

David beheaded Goliath. Imagine a young boy walking around with a head of an enemy in his hands chanting praises to God. To behead an enemy meant to strip an enemy of all powers. Incidentally, when Saul died he was beheaded, and his body was hung up in the place of a false god named Dagon.

David died of old age and in riches and honor. Saul died a miserable death and his body without proper burial. He was shown to be conquered by an evil spirit, because God wanted to show the people where disobedience can lead to.

Spiritual warfare can be intense and frightening at times as the enemy seeks to advance and take territory from us, particularly the territory of our mind. The mind governs all that is within us. It is the motherboard of our life's function. We can either break down mentally or survive and thrive mentally. How we respond is a matter of how we find strength and iron will.

Spiritual warfare can take its toll on you It can exhaust your soul. David was a warrior, and David was used to battling; those battles were spiritual. Because those enemies had a spiritual gripe against David's people, it was the conflict of the gods. Between Yahweh and that of the heathen. Israel was God's chosen seed. When you are chosen you will be hated on.

So these battles for David were spiritual, incited by demons, big and small. They exhausted his soul, but they were meaningful, nonetheless. Understand,all battles mean something in the spirit, so you have to be able to discern when you are fighting what really is on the line

"After David had finished talking with Saul, he met Jonathan, the king's son. There was an immediate bond between them, for Jonathan loved David. From that day on Saul kept David with him and wouldn't let him return home. And Jonathan made a solemn pact with David, because he loved him as he loved himself. Jonathan sealed the pact by taking off his robe and giving it to David, together with his tunic, sword, bow, and belt" (1 Samuel 18: 1-4).

Chapter 5

More than Friends, We're Blood Brothers

To have true friendship, is sacred, especially over the bond of peace. However, David was a blood brother to Jonathan and Jonathan a blood brother to David. They were bound by covenant. And it meant both parties taking risks to be friends. Jonathan's father was jealous of David.His victories in the time of war had propelled him into notoriety and fame. The people loved David.They had become familiar with him and his exploits.

Jonathan knew that David was a sure king, and even though Jonathan was to inherit the throne, he surrendered to God's will. Sometimes things don't go according to plan and one has to be flexible enough and humble enough to bend towards the direction God is moving Jonathan would've thrown a temper tantrum, and he could have become an enemy of David because of David's blessing inconveniencing him. Instead, he became a blood brother to David.

It's rare to see someone genuinely happy for you. It's rare to see someone happy with no reservations in their heart or qualms about your success and your season of blessing. It's rare to have someone promote you with no ulterior motive of their own, and this was Jonathan.

He helped David on his road to success. He went against his dad when he was in the wrong for David. He risked his life for him as well, almost being pinned to a wall by a javelin launched at him in rage because he was on David's side and wanted to see him succeed.

When you find a devoted friend, trust them. If they are interested in you and love you with their heart, as Jonathan did towards David, appreciate the gift God has given you and be faithful towards them. Friendship like that is hard to find. Jonathan was key to David's success and there will be people that are key to your life destiny and will unlock the portals of blessing in your life because God has positioned them to do so.

If it wasn't for Jonathan, David would not have gotten as far as he did. It was Jonathan's love for David, and the fact that he loved the righteousness of David, that moved him to help him. Sometimes, people will see good in you, and it's because God has permitted them to see it and that makes them support you and choose you. Where on the other hand, no matter what you say or do others are blind to your goodness.

Jonathan was more than a friend to David; he was his blood brother. They say, "blood is thicker than water," a cliche for the solidarity of family over friends But in David's case it was not his family that was behind him, it was a friend, and "there is a friend that sticks closer than a brother" as the Bible says.

And it makes me think that when that was penned, the relationship of Jonathan and David came to the mind of the writer of that Proverb. So we need a companion when ascending to higher heights, and for David it was his throne. However, when we get there, we must remember their help and assistance and not suffer from selective amnesia when it comes to who did what for us.

> When the victorious Israelite army was returning home after David had killed the Philistine, women from all the towns of Israel came out to meet King Saul. They sang and danced for joy with tambourines and cymbals. This was their song: "Saul has killed his thousands, and David his ten thousands!" This made Saul very angry. "What's this?" he said. "They credit David with ten thousands and me with only thousands. Next they'll be making him their king!" So from that time on Saul kept a jealous eye on David" (1 Samuel 18:6-9).

Chapter 6

Tried by the Most Vehement Flames

David was tried by the fire after his victory over Goliath. He was hounded by Saul for what some scholars say was years before his ascension to the throne. It seems like this hounding was done because Saul was jealous of the praises David had received and accolades from the people after the huge victory over the champion of Gath known as Goliath.

It's amazing how people will be jealous of you when they fail to do what you do. Saul would've won the battle because the confrontation was spiritual, and if he had the courage to confront the spiritual battle, Yahweh would've given him the battle. The whole battle was over the name of God and his people. However, Saul was not courageous enough to fight the fight and let a stranger come in and fight the battle.

If you don't stay courageous, someone else will. David developed courage while tending the goats and the sheep. He had to be protective and even combative. God was preparing him for his fight with Goliath, because Goliath would be a critical win for the people. It would put the Philistines into servitude of Israel and propel the fighter into notoriety. It's necessary that we fight some battles because they are key in the spiritual realm and will put us in notoriety in the spirit.

Goliath was a Nephilim spirit a hybrid of a man, a representative of Evil, while David a representative of righteousness. Saul was jealous and furious because he could not play this role. His heart was not as David's. Certain types of heart fight certain battles because the soul of a man is demonstrated when challenged. When Saul was presented the challenge, his heart and soul could not meet the challenge because he was a coward.

A true man can meet the challenges of life. He does not have to be violent or have machismo, but he must be able to meet challenges with the help of God. Saul was no longer helped by God; he was slowly but surely losing his throne, because God had ordained it so, that one that who was "after his own heart" would be the leader of his people .

And so, Saul attacked David, because David reflected to him his failure and his mistakes as a king. He pursued David. And it was during this time, David would pen the sweetest Psalms and would be known as the "sweet psalmist of Israel." But wait, how can tribulation be sweet? It is sweet when the Lord is involved in it and when you come out on the other side of it because of the Lord .

The fire of tribulation can be painful and can make one plea to God for help, and sometimes God will not deliver until the process is over. The fire is meant to purge and urge one to righteousness and a clearer picture of God and His way. No doubt, sometimes God's way is unorthodox. He moves from the left side rather than the right side,making him strange and aloof to one's plight.But in actuality, it is a manifestation of his love from the left side .

So, the name David means "Beloved," and truly he was beloved by God and the people. It is good to be loved by the people you will lead. There can be a sense of loyalty in that regard. Of course, there are enemies who will try to take away from your leadership, but the people manifested their love when David was in the most despondent state, running from a mad and confused king who was obsessed with killing a Shepherd boy that God was obviously pleased with. God put David on the run, and it seemed as if he was furthest from the throne when all this was happening.

Saul had an easy road to the throne. David came to ascension by way of difficulty. Difficulty is divine at times. It is God's means of proving that you have been selected. It's never really ever pleasant, but it is God's way of ensuring that you have been chosen and revealing why you have been chosen. The difficulty makes you and is never meant to break you. When David would have rest from his enemies, it would bring joy to his soul.

Truly God was with David in the hills and in the low land as he ran from Saul's senseless manhunt. He escaped the javelin and thousands of footmen pursuing him. He had the respect of a ruler before ever having securing the throne or the riches of a monarch. But God was making him rich in his soul. How can one be made rich in his soul? Only by the fire of the Lord that purges the soul. Saul did not have that benefit, because he did not have that favor from God. Difficulty when in service to God proves His favor on your life: the benefits are immense and precious.

The fire is violent at times, so violent that it could be Terrorizing. Jesus said, "The kingdom of heaven suffers violence but the violent take it by force." So, those who serve God will be persecuted but it is those who are resistant towards violence of evil that will achieve and receive the kingdom of God! And David surely was resistant and strong, never completely caving into the persecution of King Saul.

David was sustained by God; His gracious provision was there with him in the fiery turbulence which he experienced. God does not promise that you will be removed from the fire, but His presence is an assurance that the fire will not consume you .

> "'Who am I, and what is my family in Israel that I should be the king's son-in-law?' David exclaimed. 'My father's family is nothing!' So when the time came for Saul to give his daughter Merab in marriage to David, he gave her instead to Adriel, a man from Meholah." (1 Samuel 18:18-19).

Chapter 7

The Pain of Rejection and Loss

So, we all know or have experienced a form of rejection and loss, whether on a macro level or micro level we have suffered pain. As a matter of fact, it's difficult to navigate this life without doing so it is inevitable. David knew the pain of loss. He was told that if he fought the Lord's battles,he would be given the king's daughter. However, after doing so, and doing so valiantly, he was robbed of the promise of Merab, and she was given to someone else.

And mind you, this other person was not on David's level. In no way was he as valiant as David, and he did not fight the Lord's battles, yet he was granted the king's daughter with the benefits of being a son in law to the king. David desired love like any man. And he was a young, charismatic man who attracted women to him. Mind you, he was a military warrior of praise that had come into notoriety with the people.

And then he is dealt a blow to his heart when he found out his potential wife is given to another man. This is rejection and loss to a high degree. I recall seeing a woman with whom I had a connection me for another man on Valentine's day. I felt so much pain, and I wept to the Lord and told him to have His way,as Is at a computer table wishing I had not given this woman my heart.

So, rejection sometimes is directed towards us, and sometimes it is Circumstantial. Whatever the case, we all are or have been victims of Rejection.But the question is, how do we deal with it? And how does the Lord use it? If it's even possible for Him to do so? The answer is yes; he can use rejection.

See, David was used to rejection. When Samuel came to anoint and sacrifice to the new king, David was not invited to the party. He was left out and thought not worthy enough to be there. David was not considered, and he was forgotten about and left to tend the sheep, which was a poor man's job. However, God's heart is with the rejected.

I think of those who are in prison. I am a former convict and I served an 8-10 year prison sentence. In prison, you are in the world of the forgotten, the condemned, the violent, the repulsive, the rejected, and the brokenhearted.

But God is behind the slabs of concrete and the razor wire. He walks the corridors of the prison halls and visits prisoners in their cells, changing and transforming their lives bye his love and power, and granting them hope of a better day to some who will never leave life in the hereafter.

God loves the rejected and exalts them as he did David. God knew what was in Saul's heart. He knew that he would never be honorable towards his words and towards David, God permitted David to go through the pain so that he would learn to trust in God, because God would never reject him and would see to it that he experienced the goodness of God when others treated him poorly.

So, he lost Merab to Adriel. However, through that he gained even more favor with God, because when you fall out of favor with man, one gains favor with God. Man's favor is short, but God's lasts a lifetime. David lived for 75 years and reigned for over 40 years, but throughout his lifetime he had the favor of the Most High!

Favor is important, because it opens doors that otherwise would not be open, and favor sends people to help you get to where you need to be when you do not know how to get there by yourself. Favor is that special grace that accompanies the blessed person, and David had special grace over his life. Even when he was rejected, he was accepted by God.

And favor can close doors as well. Certain people that should be out of your life, God will remove so that you stay blessed. Even though David did not get Merab, it was all in the sovereign hands of God, meaning God knew what Saul would do. He knew that Saul would lie to David, that he was looking to set him up for failure. And even though David did not get the prize, he never failed when Saul challenged him under false pretensees .

And this showed Saul that God was with him and provoked him to fear and concern. (Caveat, whenever your enemies are confused and their plots are foiled, you have the favor of God). Whenever they test you and you pass, you are succeeding because God is with you, and one should be humble. You don't want to fall out of favor with the source of your blessings as Saul fell out of favor with God and lost his kingdom to a better man than he because of disobedience .

Disobedience will lead to God rejecting you. He may cause you to lose some things to get you to repent. I've had great blessings from God, yet because of disobedience they were taken away from me. But God is so merciful that after repentance, one can get his blessings back.

He is truly a Heavenly Father and will reward and discipline as a Heavenly Father should. Jesus called God a Father, but God is a spirit that has birthed us into his family making us sons and daughters of God. We cry Abba, meaning daddy, an affectionate term for Him in a loving relationship.

And God was a Heavenly Father for David, a better father than his earthly dad, who also rejected and did not see the king in David. Sometimes, when people reject us it's because they are blind to who and what we are. Sometimes, we are blind to who we are ,and it takes someone else to reveal it. David didn't see himself as a king; neither did his family. However, Samuel came to reveal that,and it was not apparent to him only by revelation of the Lord .

Because the Lord weighs the heart...the Egyptians were of the belief the heart was to be weighed in the afterlife in order to continue on to joy, happiness, and family. The heart was to be weighed against the weight of a feather, and if it was light then it would pass the test, but if it was found heavy with the weight of sin then it would be forever an inhabitant of the underworld of the dead.

Similarly, God weighs our hearts and knows what is in them, and can discern our true self by testing our hearts. Nothing is hidden from Him. It may be hidden from man, but never from him.

"But one day when Saul was sitting at home, with spear in hand, the tormenting spirit from the LORD suddenly came upon him again. As David played his harp,

> Saul hurled his spear at David. But David dodged out of the way, and leaving the spear stuck in the wall, he fled and escaped into the night" (1 Samuel 19:9-10).

Chapter 8
Dodging Javelins in the Night

David was seeking to help Saul. He was seeking to use one of his gifts to help soothe the relentless and tormenting feeling Saul was experiencing because he fell out of favor with God. David was a musician and had used his gift of music to help Saul in the past.

As a matter of fact, when Saul and the people around him were at a loss, someone recommended David, having seen him on the harp. It's amazing how "your gifts will make room for you, as the Bible says, because David found himself in the king's court.

However, just as your gift will make room for you, they will also get you in trouble, especially when the beneficiary is ungrateful. You will be dodging arrows in the night. Why was Saul so angry? Why did he try to pierce his help to the wall with a javelin?

Sometimes God allows this to show you the harsh reality of service. Service is not always a pleasant thing because sometimes the people you serve are unthankful, violent, and even murderous. And you must realize that you do not do it because of them, although there may be compassion involved but you do it as an offering unto God.

People will use you. Jesus said, "pray for them that despite fully use you," because the nature of man is a posture of ingratitude even when you have gone all out to help them, they will hurl javelins at you, metaphorically speaking. Why bother one may ask? Because it is the road of the righteous.

David was trying to help. Even after Saul was clearly not good to him, he sought to give him the "benefit of the doubt"and help him. This is an example of what it means to love others and God. The ministry has its rewards, but it also has the story of the ungrateful.

Some people will not receive and will not be thankful. It is at that time you must evaluate your motivation for service.

Service takes the spotlight off of you and onto another. One cannot be self centered or selfish in the ministry. David exerted his enemy to help a pitiful and foolish king through song (Caveat, music is spiritual, and depending on the heart behind the music, one can invite certain spirits to inhabit your music, making the atmosphere very spiritual).

However, in the case of David, there were times he could calm the turbulence with music and other times he could not. In this case, the spirit that was troubling Saul was so much of a problem that it sought to move him to kill David. Think about it, the spirit was trying to stow away with the answer to the problem, which was David and his music.

Sometimes, when someone is dominated by an evil spirit the spirit pushes away the answer. Jesus casted out a demon from the man who lived among the dead in the Gadarenes. After he was done, the people wanted him out. Jesus helped solve a problem that they were having. Yet, the people, instead of being thankful and offering him praise, wanted the messiah out so he left.

In the same way, David, through his music, was dealing with an evil spirit in Saul. Saul wanted David dead in return for his help. This is what happens where there is demonic stronghold. It's never easy to get the demonic to give up residence or to leave. What happened to David when he had to dodge javelins in the night indicates what one can be up against when trying to serve.

To further illustrate my point, there is the story of Reverend Paul Jones, a dynamic gospel singer and preacher who was from Texas. At the height of his ministry, he was known for the song "I Won't

Complain" when some men that he once ministered to shot and killed him in a robbery.

Sometimes, the people we help can turn on us as did Saul when he hurled javelins at David in the night, and David had to flee from his presence.

But God was with David. Even when a raging and delusional king sought to hurt him, God was with him,providing divine protection. Saul never could hurt David. He made attempts on his life. But he never could be successful in his plans against David, because he was coming against the God he belonged to

> Then Saul sent troops to watch David's house. They were told to kill David when he came out the next morning. But Michal, David's wife, warned him, "If you don't escape tonight, you will be dead by morning." So she helped him climb out through a window, and he fled and escaped. Then she took an idol and put it in his bed, covered it with blankets, and put a cushion of goat's hair at its head. When the troops came to arrest David, she told them he was sick and couldn't get out of bed. But Saul sent the troops back to get David. He ordered, "Bring him to me in his bed so I can kill him!" 16 But when they came to carry David out, they discovered that it was only an idol in the bed with a cushion of goat's hair at its head. "Why have you betrayed me like this and let my enemy escape?" Saul demanded of Michal. "I had to," Michal replied. "He threatened to kill me if I didn't help him" (1 Samuel 19:11-17).

Chapter 9
She's a Life Saver

So, David has another shot at love but its not without turmoil and trouble. Michal becomes a lifesaver. On a fateful night, he flees her home as a band of troops come to look for him so that Saul can personally kill him. Michal urges him to leave and put a mannequin in the bed, along with some goat hair to deceive the troops into thinking that David is sick and bedridden.

Needless to say, she is smart. Later on in David's life, God would curse her and shut up her womb after she would ridicule King David for praising the Lord in an undignified way as he danced naked before the Lord with all his might. (Caveat, this says something about the Lord. That with Him, when you are right, you are right, and when you are wrong, you are wrong. He is not a respecter of persons in judgement).

And yes, he remembers what you did yesterday, but he also is mindful of what you do today. Michael Jackson had a song called "Remember the Time." It was a love ballad of recalling one's first time meeting someone and falling in love

Michal did save David's life, and David was most certainly grateful for that. Their relationship surely suffered from outside trouble. David could not much as eat a meal in peace without worrying about Saul head hunting him.

What's it like to be a woman with a man that the government is after? It must have been a stress on that relationship and surely God rewarded Michal, the wife of the anointed and new found king. And surely her commitment to David in that hour was tested.

But I can't" get the fact that God would later shut up her womb for

Ridiculing David out of my mind. One act of kindness or mercy does not qualify you for a lifetime of blessings with the Lord; it seems like she was with David all the way to the point of putting her own self at risk.

When I used to conduct weddings, the best part was the vows, watching the emotion on the newlywed's faces as they exchanged vows and looked in each others eyes as if piercing the soul and asking and declaring to be together until death do us part.

And David needed a significant other that would be with him until the end, even if the end meant her life or his. There is something about trouble that can either bring one closer or further apart, and in this instance, they were brought closer as death loomed over their life and relationship.

And God did grace her with the intellect and wisdom to help David. She was a quick thinker. She was quick on her feet as she decided what to say to the band of men that came to her place that night.

When choosing a spouse, one must look at all aspects of their being before uniting. See, the body is just the house that houses the soul, but it's the soul that is the person! Looks are of minimal value when you are in trouble, and in David's case, when your life is on the line.

But wit and smarts are not the same as wisdom. If Michal was wise, she would have recognized that David was praising the Lord when we witness David's" joy in bringing back the ark of the covenant! However, she tampered with the Lord's praise.

And God will never allow you to tamper with His praise. We should be careful not to critique others in church who come to church with boisterous and exuberant praise that is less stoic than ours, because that praise belongs to God and we should not tamper with it. It's the Lord's.

They say, "you can't look a gift horse in the mouth"and that "no one is perfect," so you must accept the good and the ugly when it comes to relationships. When it comes to the Bible, the characters are laid bare for the naked eye to see and assess the flaws and beauties of their character. It's a historical book and meant to be an honest book.

Michal had more courage than most women. She loved David enough to risk her life. She didn't want to see the man she loved lose his life because of a jealous and insecure king. And she wanted her relationship to work as most women do. Her hopes were that the trouble would subside, but when you are married to an anointed person, trouble will come to your house!

So, the question then is, how do you deal with it, because there is no training manual on what to do when you are with an anointed person, Yes, they are a blessing but even more they are always under attack!

> "David replied, 'Tomorrow we celebrate the new moon festival. I've always eaten with the king on this occasion, but tomorrow I'll hide in the field and stay there until the evening of the third day'" (1 Samuel 20:5).

Chapter 10
The New Moon Festival

The new moon festival was a time during the first of the month, where sacrifice of all kinds would be given unto the Lord. Goats would be sacrificed and drink offerings, as well as other cattle. So why was this time mentioned in the Bible when David was dealing with the vengeance of King Saul? And it really wasn't vengeance at all to be honest, but it was a satanic attack on David and the position God was leading him to.

Why is it mentioned? Well, my thoughts on it are that sometimes God does not want physical sacrifice but spiritual sacrifice. God is a consuming fire that burns away the fat and roast his sacrifice to his delight. David's life was meant to be a sacrifice, and as he ran from Saul, God was purging something from his character.

Understand that when the pressures of life get intense, God is looking for a sacrifice. And he is not using a priest anymore to shed the blood of sacrifice for sins or for celebratory purposes but will use a fiery trial or fiery trials to get the offering he desires. Picture the crackling of fire and the smell of charcoal and smoke filling the air as game roasts upon an open fire.

This is what God seeks to do in the trials we go through. And he is still a God that desires sacrifice: the giving up of something to make the quality purer and better is delightful to God. It is our reason for worship.

It was the purge that is needed. As things got intense for David, God was setting ablaze all the fat off of David's life, the fat of pride and self dependency. It is God's festival, a celebratory thing in the eyes of God.

Angels in heaven rejoice when we go through our trials, not sadistically, but to know that God is making us better is a delight to them. They comfort us as well and let us know that "all things are working together for our good."

Welcome to God's new moon festival, where the new day is celebrated by sacrifice, a new time ushered in by the festivities of life. Some say David fled the pursuit of Saul for ten years, some say even more. But God was preparing his sacrifice, a sweet and smelling savor to his senses, in putting David through the test. David went through it because God loved David.

Some of us have different roads in life. Saul had an easy road to the throne, but David's was very difficult, filled with intrigue and intensity, hardship and delay. The question is, why did God do that? It's because he loved David that He was personally inviting him to His new moon festivities, by asking him not to bring a sacrifice but to become a sacrifice.

There comes a time in every man or woman's life that you must not bring a sacrifice, but become one. Jesus became a sacrifice for sin of all humanity and we too must learn to be a sacrifice.

So, David learns to have God's holy fire vehemently burn away his character flaws in the heat of God's affliction. After all, he was going to be a king and God was going to groom him for the position personally.

There is no telling how God will groom you for the position. Once He's called for the position, we don't always come ready. But be sure, if God has called you He will prep you for success.

Because God doesn't desire your failure, but that you might bring Him glory and participate in that glory to the joy of your own soul and to the execution of God's will on earth as it is in heaven.

In this society that we live in, sacrifice can be foreign to us, because we are always asking and not giving up anything. We always have our hand out to receive and not to release! In the fire of God's new moon festival, we have things burned away from us, a pleasing aroma to God, a fragrance of love and worship.

In this day and age, God is still in the business of sacrifice. No sacrifice will out do the sacrifice of Jesus, but all sacrifices are meant to make us more like Jesus.

If we only will allow Him to do His perfect work in us we shall go deeper into spiritual things when we learn how to suffer with Him. We participate in God's New Moon Festival

> Saul boiled with rage at Jonathan. "You stupid son of a whore!" he swore at him. "Do you think I don't know that you want him to be king in your place, shaming yourself and your mother? As long as that son of Jesse is alive, you'll never be king. Now go and get him so I can kill him!" "But why should he be put to death?" Jonathan asked his father. "What has he done?" Then Saul hurled his spear at Jonathan, intending to kill him. So at last Jonathan realized that his father was really determined to kill David. Jonathan left the table in fierce anger and refused to eat on that second day of the festival, for he was crushed by his father's shameful behavior toward David (1st Samuel 20:30-33).

Chapter 11

Non Opportunist Heart

We speak much about David and his heart towards God, but very little is said about the heart of Jonathan. He too was a man after God's own heart. The record of the Bible may not state it, but what's recorded are his actions, and by them we can discern his heart.

Now Jonathan was by right successor to be king, because he was the son of Saul, so he was already a prince of prince David is anointed to be king, this should have been concerning to Jonathan, because it would mean David stood as a threat to his future blessings. However, Jonathan is not concerned about a crown but saving the head of David from the murderous plot of his father.

He obviously felt that David was a good man and that he did not deserve to die. He didn't care about power as much as he cared about his friendship to David. And Jonathan surrendered to the idea of David being King as if he felt David was a better man.

Jonathan was not an opportunist by any stretch. He was a man of wise Judgement, realizing God had chosen David for the greater position, but it does not mean that Jonathan was not great himself.

Jonathan could have helped his Father to seize and kill David because he was a threat to the kingdom's power being anointed to be king. Instead, he sees David as a good man and his Father as a senseless murderer.

It could be that as he was next in line, he did not want the power. However, I see it as he surrendered to God's will and helped David to become king.

Jonathan's name means, "Yahweh has given" and truly God had given him a true friend in David, but also Yahweh had given him a non opportunistic heart, where he did not seek power for himself.

And he was wise enough to know whether he had a good friend or not in David. When I was a child and we would meet someone we liked, the next step was to ask, "Do you want to be my friend?" Today, people don't value or understand friendship.

Friendship is sacred, and it's good to have someone to accompany you in this journey called life. It's good for people to not see what they can get out of you but what they can give to you as a testament to their devotion to your friendship.

The world is as if you are swimming in the water with sharks and you must learn how to swim to make it, or else you will be savagely eaten up, and King Saul was a shark that sought to destroy David But Jonathan was the lifeguard who saved him.

It's easy to make an acquaintance, but in this pilgrim journey we have few companions and guides that help get to our destination and there are many detours on destination road. King Saul was one of them for David, but Jonathan was a companion to David for as long as he had life in him, he would make sure David was where he needed to be.

It was an opportunity for Jonathan to show integrity, integrity his father did not have. If his father had integrity and humbled himself, God would've dealt with him much differently, but it was destined for Saul's life to end the way it did.

It was destined for David to be king after Saul was deposed, but it was also destined for Jonathan to help him get there, and on the day of judgement, Jonathan will be rewarded by God for helping David get to where he needed to be, by the selfless act of surrendering his right to the will of God.

Saul was the epitome of selfishness and Jonathan the epitome of selflessness, and selfishness is an ugly trait to have no matter what the situation or scenario is, while selflessness is the standard of God. It's funny Jonathan had the same genetic makeup as his Father but not the same heart .

So, a person can have family but not be like family and "blood is not always thicker than water." God calls us out of certain things and ties and even causes some family members to stand out above the rest. That's why some are the first to get a degree in their home, or first to acquire wealth or have a successful marriage.

Jonathan stood out as a loyal man, and his Father was disloyal because David was of service to Saul helping him by playing the harp to soothe his torments from spirits, battling his battles, becoming his armor bearer, etc. Yet Saul was disloyal after David had exerted so much energy helping him, and anytime one finds loyalty it's not to be taken for granted, as in the case of Jonathan and David.

But God has a way of supplying what is needed at different intervals of time. That is why we should and can depend on Him. In the life and case of David, Jonathan was a gift of God which is what his name means to David and to his future.

> "I only have the sword of Goliath the Philistine, whom you killed in the valley of Elah," the priest replied. "It is wrapped in a cloth behind the ephod. Take that if you want it, for there is nothing else here." "There is nothing like it!" David replied. "Give it to me!" (1st Samuel 21:9).

Chapter 12
Victories of the Valley

In David's famous psalm he says, "yea though I walk the valley of the shadow of death I will fear no evil," and I am persuaded that David was being mindful of the time he entered the valley of Elah to face Goliath, the Philistine who was a champion of military might.

We often speak of the valley as low and dark places but not as places of victory. But God is God of the hills and of the valleys. David had God with him as he entered the valley of Elah. He had God's presence.

In today's world, people are purchasing books on how to be successful. And in these books, they learn to practice their own presence so that as they walk into a room they can feel empowered.

However, not too many people can sense the presence of God in their life circumstances. When David was on the run, he sought food and help. There was the bread of presence and the sword of Goliath wrapped in the ephod.

David grabbed the sword, the sword symbolized great victory and a token of remembrance of what exactly God had done in the valley. In life, we will face many valleys, and in those valleys we will win, because God's holy presence accompanies us. However, we must secure the tokens of remembrance. And for David, it was the sword of Goliath, and it served as a reminder of what God had done before and what God would do again.

The victory in Elah was spiritual for David because Goliath came against the God of Israel, and David met the challenge in the name of Yahweh. Some valleys are deeply dark and spiritual. The conquering of Goliath was equivalent to defeating the Devil. The champion had incited fear in Israel's military army for a span of 40 days, and when

David showed up he had met the challenge. The interesting thing was that he was not part of the military regime.

God used someone uncertified and unsanctioned to win the battle, some one not trained in conventional warfare David had only the training as a Shepherd boy who engaged in protecting the sheep from lions and bears.

Understand that when God calls you or plans to use you, he may train you in ways that are not the norm for unusual victories in the valley, because in the valley there are the strangest battles to be fought. The valley represents the need to trust in God more than ever.

So David carries the sword of Goliath to defend himself, and he finds himself in yet another valley. This time, it's because the king of Israel is jealous of him and sees him as a threat to his powers, powers that are failing because of his disobedience to God that ended in the pronouncement of him losing his kingdom.

David understood the importance of the presence of God, while Saul understood it as well but Saul understood it as a thing that would escape him no matter how hard he tried to grasp it after it was made known that God had found a better man for the kingship.

David understood the value of God's presence, to have God surround one with favor, accompany one on their journey, and to impress oneself upon another is a powerful thing

David would later sin but never lose the presence. King Saul would sin but would lose the presence. And that was the deciding factor in who he would be. A man without the presence of God is the most miserable sight and to be pitied. But a man with the presence of God is the most delightful sight to behold and walks in power and honor.

"So David left Gath and escaped to the cave of Adullam. Soon his brothers and all his other relatives joined him there. Then others began coming - men who were in trouble or in debt or who were just discontented until David was the captain of about 400 men" (1 Samuel 22:1-2).

Chapter 13

My Adullam Cave

The word Adullam means refuge or hiding place and when David was on the run. Adullam became a safe house for him. Surely, he needed a place to hide from the ferocious pursuit of King Saul. And he was joined by those whom the Bible says "discontented" the oppressed in the number of 400 men, including his own family.

We all need a place of refuge, a place to hide from the pressures of Life. For some, it will be your local church where the fellowship keeps one encouraged and is sweet. For some, it will be God Himself as the Bible says, "the name of the lord is a strong tower that the righteous run into and is safe."

I recall a time in my life when I backslid and needed time to regroup, collect myself, and find peace again. I needed shelter from the rain in my life, and I found a fellow pastors church to be my place of refuge temporarily as I got myself together in God.

The Bible mentions that those who were with David were the down trodden and the oppressed. It seems like they could identify with him and his present struggle. And in life, we need someone or a group of persons we can identify with. That David could identify with his people created a love for King David.

When we are going through hardship, we don't just need a place to hide. We need people that understand us and will not judge us as we attempt to discern the will of God in our lives and understand ourselves in the matter we are dealing with.

And David and his men at Adullam had an understanding that they both needed each other and a place to hide. (Caveat, it's interesting that David's family is also mentioned. It seems as if Saul may not have made good on his promises towards David's family when it was said that he who would beat Goliath his family would be free in Israel because his family joined him in distress. Nevertheless, there was an Adullam cave, a place of refuge, a place to hide. This causes me to think of a time I was homeless on the streets, hungry, and cold. When you don't have shelter, one is without the necessities of life. And David was without shelter, but Adullam was a safe house for him, a place to be free from the trouble around him.

Jesus is our Adullam cave and his love is our shelter from the torrential storms that life will send our way in various seasons. We need a place to hide no matter how strong or intelligent we feel that we are, we need a place to hide.

Humanity is fragile, and the troubles of this life are inevitable, so it makes sense that at some point we will be overwhelmed by the issues of life and no man or woman is so strong as to deal with our problems alone, so we need the community of Adullam.

David had a community of people that were just like him, and this is the community of Adullam, a group of people that were oppressed and seeking change. And in today's world, we are tired of bad politics, race hate, and false promises, lack of income, jobs, and injustice in the judicial system. This is the community of Adullam, the same community David sought to find refuge within.

"Why have you and the son of Jesse conspired against me?" Saul demanded. "Why did you give him food and a sword? Why have you consulted God for him? Why have you encouraged him to kill me, as he is trying to do this very day?" "But sir," Ahimelech replied, "is anyone among all your servants as faithful as David, your son-in-law? Why, he is the captain of your bodyguard and a highly honored member of your household! This was certainly not the first time I had consulted God for him! May the king not accuse me and my family in this matter, for I knew nothing at all of any plot against you." "You will surely die,

Ahimelech, along with your entire family!" the king shouted. And he ordered his bodyguards, "Kill these priests of the Lord, for they are allies and conspirators with David! They knew he was running away from me, but they didn't tell me!" But Saul's men refused to kill the Lord's priests. Then the king said to Doeg, "You do it." So Doeg the Edomite turned on them and killed them that day, eighty-five priests in all, still wearing their priestly garments (1 Samuel 22:13-18).

Chapter 14

A Sacrilegious Heart

Sacrilege is a disposition and manner of disrespect towards what is Holy, divine, and sacred. King Saul was sacrilegious. He did not respect what was holy. And he did not respect God. He was so far away from God that he was doomed to die the way in which he did. In his rage, he had the priest of the Lord murdered and as he interrogated them, they appealed to his senseless rage by commenting on the faithfulness of David. They used his character to show Saul how wrong he was for seeking David's life.

And when Saul had appealed to his bodyguards, they would not touch Ahimelech and the priest because they recognized the moral error King Saul was in. That is why Doeg the Edomite ended doing Saul's evil bidding.

And in today's time the world can be sacrilegious. There is no respect for people of the Lord, neither is there reverence for what is holy or God himself, which is declaration of hard heartedness and lack of faith. The spirit of Edom is upon the people and is alive and well even in the church.

There is regard for who and what are set apart. David was not like that. He had respect, and he was the complete polar opposite of Saul. The Bible contrasts this to show why God chose David and just exactly why he deemed David "a man after His own heart."

It seems like God put David through this difficulty to make sitting on the throne worthwhile, because Saul did not have the same pathway toward the monarchy. And it seems like God tests those he loves, as if the testing is a gift. One may reject that notion, but even Jesus said persecution was a gift or blessing, so David was persecuted for being God's man.

Expect trouble, senseless and out of the ordinary trouble, if you are God's man or God's woman, because men and Satan will make it hard for you to succeed. But it is these moments that shape a person and make them have iron in their spirit and produce steel in their character.

We are sometimes anointed but too soft for the role we are called to play, so there is a toughening up period that we go through. David had many battles he was going to fight in the future, and he was going to have to learn how to navigate his life without breaking down.

How do we avoid the breakdown? Surely it is by God's grace and provision that we deal with the enemy's onslaught. However, there is a matter of the will and one must be strong in his or her will to endure the hardship that is attached to blessing.

So, King Saul was a weak man He did not come from a position of strength when dealing with David. Sin makes a man weak, and righteousness makes a man strong.

And in his weakness, he was sacrilegious and lost reverence for God and holy things.

> "Saul soon learned that David was at Keilah . 'Good!' He exclaimed. 'We've got him now! God has handed him over to me for he has trapped himself in a walled town!" (1 Samuel 23:7).

Chapter 15
Delusional Thoughts

There are some people that have the attitude or the notion that God is with them and supports their bad behavior. I have times in my life where I backslid, still a child of God, but in sin.

Certainly, God had mercy on me and helped me to get back to a right relationship with Him. Unfortunately, there are those that are in rebellion against God and feel that God is still with them.

They point to the anointing and to their spiritual exploits. Yet, God is not pleased with them because their hearts are not right, and He is against them as he was against Saul. There was a time the Spirit of the Lord was with Saul, but once it departed he became a miserable man.

I won't lie, there was a time I fell away from the Lord and thought I could still preach and teach God's word effectively. I thought I could still operate in the anointing, and to a degree I did. But I soon was entangled in the cords of sin.

I sought God and others for help, and so God had mercy on me and got me back on track. The moral of the story is that it is a lie from the pits of hell to feel like God can still be with you in your disobedience, and this was the case for Saul. He thought he could attack God's man and still be blessed.

And he thought he could still be king when God and the prophet Samuel turned their backs on him because of his disobedience and deviant behavior,and God is no respecter of persons. He dealt with David and his treacherous sins of adultery and murder. The difference between Saul and David is that David was of humble heart and truly penitent, while Saul was prideful and seeking to save his position and to save face.

God does not condone sin, and neither will He bless it. Because he is holy and respects principal and is the epitome of principal. Saul did not respect principals because his power got to his head, which is what occurs with most political leaders of today. The idea of power intoxicates them and causes them to not see that they have been blessed by God to be in their position and that they are accountable to God in it as well.

> "Now's your opportunity!" David's men whispered to him. "Today the Lord is telling you, 'I will certainly put your enemy into your power, to do with as you wish.'" So David crept forward and cut off a piece of the hem of Saul's robe. But then David's conscience began bothering him because he had cut Saul's robe. He said to his men, "The Lord forbid that I should do this to my lord the king. I shouldn't attack the Lord's anointed one, for the Lord himself has chosen him." So David restrained his men and did not let them kill Saul (1 Samuel 24:4-7).

Chapter 16

My Conscience Is My Light

In life we need a guide on our decisions. And sometimes that guidance will come from books, church friends, and family. However, if we do not have those outlets, our conscience is our guide. Our conscience is formed or influenced by our family, upbringing, culture, education, etc.

Some of us go against our conscience, and it becomes hardened, cold, and numb. We can lose our conscience but we can get it back by heeding it and being sensitive to it. Our conscience is our inner light and our moral compass helping us to conduct ourselves in a manner that complies with the moral rules of our society.

It is innate and inherent. However, our consciences may be different based on how we came up and the makings of our persona and schema. Nevertheless, it is meant to guide us to a clearer pathway of light and clarity towards our decision-making.

David had a conscience, and towards his sworn enemy he heeded it. Saul was pursuing him and David and his men came upon him in a very vulnerable situation. David's men felt that it was of God that David's relentless enemy be found to be killed. However, David cut the piece of his robe. And this was a temptation for David to show Saul how he could have ended his life, but immediately David's conscience struck him!

The conscience of his men was not stricken, but the conscience of David was because David was hardwired to be obedient to God. Now, hard wiring is a strange thing, because it is a permanent programming of someone or something. David was permanently a person with a good conscience.

Now that does not mean he had no sin, but what it does mean is that he was a righteous man who sometimes did unrighteous things. But for the most part, he was guided by his inner alert system of right and wrong. And he did not deal with his enemy. Although he had justifiable reasons to do so, because he knew that if it was God's will, that the Lord would help him

David had respect for God. He knew that God was allowing this for a reason and that there was a bigger scheme to it than what meets the eye. He already had the blessed assurance that he would be king, and he knew he did not have to rush the process or take matters into his own hands, and that even though Saul did not behave like the Lord's anointed he would.

See, sometimes in life we cannot predict the behavior of others and neither control them, and we may not get what we expect. But we should not let the behavior of others dictate our behavior, especially in matters of obedience to God's will in a matte.

Even though David veered from his pathway, his conscience brought him back on track. And he could visibly see the wrongful actions as wrong. No one had to tell him, but his moral compass guided him! This made David par excellence as a future leader of the people, because he could be trusted to do the right thing in any given situation.

Now David was a holy man, just and righteous in a time where people appreciated those qualities more, especially when they were found in leaders of authority. True, Saul was a failure at exemplifying those qualities, but it only highlighted David's more.

One must be able to see the qualities in you that make you a leader in order to approve of your position and be influenced by your qualities. People follow good leadership with a sense of direction and

David used his internal light, also known as the conscious, to lead the people.

It was because of his conscience that he stepped in to defend his father's sheep from the lion and the bear. Because at a young age, he was a good shepherd. In his youthfulness, he could have been distracted by the things that distract young people, but he decided that for conscience sake he would be a good Shepherd God needed someone like that on the throne, who would lead the people with his moral compass.

> "Now Samuel died, and all Israel gathered for his funeral . They buried at his house in Ramah . Then David. Moved down to the wilderness of Maon" (1 Samuel 25:1).

Chapter 17
The Inevitability of Death

So, we all know that death is our exit out of this life, but we do not know when we will make that exit or how we will make that exit. No matter how great or small we are, we die. Some losses are extremely painful because of the impact an individual may have had in this life.

Samuel was a great prophet. He was dedicated to the Lord as a child and raised in the house of a holy man named Eli. In that house he learned to discern the voice of God, and knowing that voice would be a sense of direction for him and the people he would be a leader of,

As leaders, we see things in people and have certain hopes. We see future leaders and to work with, hoping that by us working with them we can fulfill the Lord's will together and see great things happen. And this was the case for Samuel and Saul.

The people wanted to be included in the number of nations that had a Monarchy, rejecting the Lord as king. Saul was then chosen but would later prove to be a failure, and this was a discouragement to him. Because he had high hopes for himself, even though the way in which he came to the throne was by the people rejecting God.

Samuel and Saul's story was of disappointment and judgement. Samuel was disappointed, but he had to pronounce God's judgement on him. And when he died, it was a devastating loss to King Saul in his need for guidance and direction.

No matter who we are. we die and partake in the curse of death brought to everyone one that would enter this cold and dreary world. There are no exemptions. Now, the Bible does mention Enoch and Elijah who were translated, but for generations and eons people parted with this life by death.

Be it a cremation or traditional funeral, you will go, but the question is in what way. Will you leave this life as a righteous person or as a wicked person? In Samuel's case he was a righteous person of the Lord. He had a relationship with God that was uncanny, because he served as a conduit of God.

It is important that we have a working knowledge of God, because He desires for us to have a connection to Him and allows us to go through this life experiencing various things that may lead us to Him. Some of us, no matter what we go through, will never end at the door of God's home. So we must take heed how we live this life and what we choose, because beyond death there is another world as we shall see later in the epic story of Saul and David.

So the prophet died, and it was a big loss to the community, Today, pastors and leaders should be involved in the communities that they are situated in. They should be beloved members of their society, impacting what is happening on a day-to-day basis.

When I was pastoring a church, I was taught by my former pastor that I should be involved in my community. And that has stayed with me until this day. We are not just called to the local church, but to the city we serve in. The light has to be shined not just in the four walls of a church building with stain glass windows and religious artifacts, but to a broader scope of where sin is present and society is decaying.

And speaking of death, there is such a thing as the death of a city the death of leadership, the death of peace, the death of love, and so on, and only the righteous can help to resurrect what is dead. So Samuel will be resurrected. He lived for God, so in judgement he will have a favorable disposition from the Lord. But even he in all his might and power will come under scrutiny.

Many of today's prophets are driven by money, the need for praise, he need to be with the in crowd by pleasing the people. Therefore, they deviate from God's words in hopes of being accepted. A true prophet will suffer tribulation, may not amass wealth, may be a thorn in the side of those in authority, and may even suffer physical harm or even death.

Today's world suffer from moral decay and only the Lords hand can heal our lands. When the moral fabric suffers from decay, we suffer from spiritual decay and need the power of God to resurrect us.

> "When Abigail saw David, she quickly got off her donkey and bowed low before him. She fell at his feet and said, "I accept all blame in this matter, my lord. Please listen to what I have to say. I know Nabal is a wicked and ill-tempered man; please don't pay any attention to him. He is a fool, just as his name suggests. But I never even saw the young men you sent'" (1Samuel 25:23-25).

Chapter 18

A Sensible Woman

David was a man prone to anger, like all of are Although very giftedand godly, there was an ugly side to David, a darker side that he did not want to come out and that others didn't want to see. We all are made up of darkness and light. This is the conflict the apostle Paul spoke of in his letter to the Romans.

However, we must learn to master our dark side and have our bodies become full of light. This can only be done by the residence of God in our lives, and even then there is tension of good versus evil and light versus darkness. I guess the reason why God loved David so much is because he struggled to see the light manifested in his life for all his life.

David was going to execute Nabal, a wealthy and wicked man who denied his humble request in his pride and condescending comments about David. But it was a woman, not just an ordinary woman but a woman of sense, who intervened in the situation and made the situation end well.

One wonders how Abigail ended up with Nabal to begin with. However, since the dawn of time there have been women that were good and wise that ended up with wicked and foolish men. Why do they stay? Only they know. However, in the case of David and Abigail she left Nabal after he died to go with David. God changed her circumstances for sure. However, it was not until after she had shown her wisdom in comparison to Nabal's folly.

She provides what Nabal would not give to David and his men which was provision for their journey and ends up in a relationship with the future king. Abigail certainly had the ability to defuse a situation and calm and angry and revenge seeking David who was about to let his darker side take over the message is that women use faculties that men do not in times of conflict and trouble, and there are women of God who know how to navigate tough waters,especially dealing with foolish husbands that seem to seek their own interest rather than the interest of their spouses.

Proverbs 31 captures the perfect picture of God's virtuous woman, and surely Abigail fits in the text as a woman of God that knows how to humble an angry man and prosper herself in the middle of it. Women are not objects for sexual gratification. And they should be evaluated for the level of good sense they possess rather than the curves of their anatomy or the looks of their faces.

A godly man needs a godly woman and vice verse, and Abigail was that woman that was sensible and smart enough to be with David, a man of character and love for God. Women should seek to model themselves after Abigail and the lesson is taught that there are those who are foolish in the world.

And no matter what you do, you can't turn a fool from his folly, only an intervention of God can do that! Surely Abigail ended up in a better situation after David had rest from his enemies and the situation of her life changed.

See, she was a king'swife and didn't even know it. Some women have settled to be with fools when they should be with wise kings. And this causes an improper balance to one's life and many regret their marriages because there is no reciprocity.

And what they give, they do not get in return and such was the case of Abigail and Nabal, but it still makes you wonder, did he become a fool after marriage or before? I believe he was a fool from the start. The seed of a fool was in him. The Bible does not discuss the circumstances in which they got married but seems like his folly had started to manifest itself after the marriage.

So did Abigail make a mistake? Yes, she did, and she stayed for her personal reasons. But even wise women make mistakes, and there are plenty of women who are sensible but living with foolish men. However, if they could've identified the seed of folly in their husbands from the beginning they would have been better positioned in life.

Some are fortunate enough to leave and find their "knight in shining armor. Some remain in an imbalanced situation. And for Abigail, David was her "knight in shining armor." God freed her from her negative situation one day when her husband was appealed to by David who was going to be king of all of Israel. And might I add she, was a blessing to David for the rest of his life because her sensibility never left her.

> Saul recognized David's voice and called out, "Is that you, my son David?" And David replied, "Yes, my lord the king. Why are you chasing me? What have I done? What is my crime? But now let my lord the king listen to his servant. If the Lord has stirred you up against me, then let him accept my offering. But if this is simply a human scheme, then may those involved be cursed by the Lord. For they have driven me from my home, so I can no longer live among the Lord's people, and they have said, 'Go, worship pagan gods.' Must I die on foreign soil, far from the presence of the Lord? Why has the king of Israel come out to search for a single flea? Why does he hunt me down like a partridge on the mountains?" Then Saul confessed, "I have sinned. Come back home, my son, and I will no longer try to harm you, for you valued my life today. I have been a fool and very, very wrong" (1Samuel 26:17-21).

Chapter 19
Socratic Questions

Socrates was the inventor of the Socratic Method, which is basically a line of questioning that has an end goal of helping the student or pupil in the classroom to arrive at learning the subject at hand. In the above passage. David questions King Saul, because much of his behavior doesn't make sense. Sometimes, the reason for irrational behavior is spiritual.

It may not be a case for medicine or counseling but a case of spiritual oppression, depression, suppression, and last but not least possession. I have to believe the devil was involved in Saul's persecution of David. He is not blatantly mentioned, but we can logically deduce that because Saul was tormented by a devil and that the devil launched a spiritual attack on David.

Think about it. David was going to lead the people with a righteous heart and hand. This would lead to properly shepherding God's flock, also known as the people of Israel, and Satan would not have wanted that. David was to be a prototype for all kings to come. Even the messiah would be called the "Son of David, "a messianic" title indeed.

So, Saul trying to eradicate David was trying to eliminate all God wanted to do through David's future reign and life. But David says some things' that describe how he viewed himself in the story. David mentions he is "a flea." In other words, he is small , tiny , insignificant, pointless to be against.

It's interesting who God raises up, how, and why, David never saw himself as legendary, even after a legendary victory over Goliath of Gath. David's humility was great, and therefore moved God to exalt him, because God is attracted to humility. God would later make David larger than life.

But David asks Saul, why the pursuit? In part, he is at a loss for it all, and in part, he is trying to show Saul how ridiculous and evil of a thing it is to use all that military might to hunt him down. He is a pauper of a man in comparison to Saul; this is how he sees himself.

Then he is comparing himself to a partridge in the mountains. Now, a partridge traditionally has been a game hunting bird. So David feels like he is part of a hunting game, that King Saul's manhunt is this relentless game where he is being hunted innocently by a jealous and ferocious King with the power to kill anytime.

The interesting thing about this is that the Lord is allowing this and has not really answered David's cry for help! It's as if the Lord is waiting for this to climax to a certain point. The Lord had knowledge David did not. Therefore, David had to operate by faith, walking into every situation not knowing futuristic details, trusting that God would help him.

The Lord was definitely operating on higher knowledge and could see how this struggle would end for David while David went from day to day wondering if it would be his last day among the living!

God was certainly in control, but there were times it did not feel like that. And this is true when we are in the midst of dark, spiritual struggle. We lose sight of the sovereignty of God. Yet His intimate knowledge we must learn to trust in.

> "But David kept thinking to himself, 'Someday Saul is going to get me. The best thing I can do is escape to the Philistines. Then Saul will stop hunting for me in Israelite territory, and I will finally be safe'" (1Samuel 27:1).

Chapter 20

Desperation

David, as a result of his need to get out of his situation, would make a desperate move to protect himself and rightfully so. As humans, self-preservation is key. We desire to put ourselves first and to survive.

Now the philistines were sworn enemies of the Israelite people. They were a pagan nation, dark, and against the God of Israel. When David fought Goliath the Philistine,he defied the David and the God of Israel which made the confrontation very spiritual.

Of course, David did valiantly by defeating their champion, even beheading him and stripping him of his powers in a triumphant win in the Valley of Elah. But now David was joining the enemy! When we are desperate, we can make poor decisions.

Our decisions say a lot about ourselves, and for the most part, David had made good choices in life good choices while serving his father Jesse good choices while serving in Saul's court. However,even a person known for good decisions can make bad decisions sometimes.

This decision of David was a decision based out of desperation. Some people get desperate and marry the wrong person. Some people get desperate and take matters off the altar of God and into their own hand. Some people get desperate and do what David did and seek covering and shelter from man rather than God.

I think the need for self preservation is innate. It is a survival mode of function that we all have. However, trusting God with our own selves is part of our worship to God. And it can be hard when we don't see God in our life circumstances or say prayers that seemingly have no response to them. But these situations arise so that we might learn to trust.

David did trust in God as we read the Psalms, some that were penned during Saul's era and the manhunts against him, and we get a look at his heart and his godliness and devotion to the things of God. And he was still a strong male, an alpha male that made seeking the face of God part of his machismo.

In a society today where people mock the servants of God. David made serving God look good. Today's man is ungodly and does not walk in high morality. Today's man is not a family man, neither will he work hard to provide. Today's man will not go to church to give God reverence. David was such an opposite of that.

David valued the presence of God, and as a matter of fact, was desperate for his spirit to abide with him David loved God. And in return he was loved by Him and showered with the favor of heaven.

> But Saul took an oath in the name of the Lord and promised, "As surely as the Lord lives, nothing bad will happen to you for doing this." Finally, the woman said, "Well, whose spirit do you want me to call up?" "Call up Samuel," Saul replied. When the woman saw Samuel, she screamed, "You've deceived me! You are Saul!" "Don't be afraid!" the king told her. "What do you see?" "I see a god coming up out of the earth," she said. "What does he look like?" Saul asked. "He is an old man wrapped in a robe," she replied. Saul realized it was Samuel, and he fell to the ground before him. "Why have you disturbed me by calling me back?" Samuel asked Saul. "Because I am in deep trouble," Saul replied. "The Philistines are at war with me, and God has left me and won't reply by prophets or dreams. So I have called for you to tell me what to do." But Samuel replied, "Why ask me, since the Lord has left you and has become your enemy? (1st Samuel 28: 10-16).

Chapter 21

The Occult War

Now, in the earlier chapter we saw that David was trying to preserve his life, before he joined the Philistines. And this was an act of self-preservation where he trusted God that the Philistines would protect him from Saul.

In this chapter, we shall cover Saul's act of desperation and see how it differs from that of David, putting Saul in a bad place with God. And David in a place of mercy with God. Now Saul goes to the witch of Endor seeking to call up Samuel for answers to his life as the throne was quickly slipping from his hands.

As a monarch of the people of Israel, he was supposed to represent God to the people. And his responsibility was to take care and govern the people of Israel by obeying God's laws and commands with the utmost respect and ensuring that the people did the same.

There were things forbidden in the law of Moses that he was to observe as part of the leading body of Israel. However, in his desperation he sought a woman with a familiar spia me A ban or a decree had gone out to stop anyone from consulting or participating in mediumship, but Saul would play the hypocrite and become two-faced and consult the witch of Endor anyway.

Now in the world today there are a host of people engaged in the Occult, from psychics, tarot cards, mediums, Santeria, Oshun, etc. And like Saul, many people are looking for answers and the answers that will sooth their curiosity. Some are in search of power and as they commit themselves to such practices they bind their soul to such things for power.

The downside is that these things are damned by the Lord and those who enter the portal of the occult find it hard to leave once they have accessed it, that is if they desire to leave it. The world is a spiritual place and we must learn how to navigate it.

However, Satan has designed traps such as the occult to destroy the lives of men by bringing them into disobedience to the Lord and a false sense of knowledge and power. David was different than Saul. Admittedly he was desperate and afraid, and he did go into enemy territory for shelter as a safe haven. However, time after time David called on God, and when his situation worsened, he continued to.

This demonstrates a continued reliance and dependence on God to turn his situation around. David never let go of his faith in God. At times, he may have fluctuated in faith but he never lost his ability to bounce back from desperation and fear. Saul, on the other hand, never really sought the merciful hand of God but continued to spiral downward in his lack of faith.

David should be emulated as a man of faith and a true warrior in more than one sense of the word, a rare gem in matters of the spirit and holiness despite his sinful mistakes. Now, the occult is a dangerous force and when Saul consulted the witch of Endor he got what he wanted in a roundabout way

Samuel appeared to him from the realm of the dead only to further condemn him. It seems like God took his disobedience very seriously and Saul's lack of repentance deepened his offence towards God. (Caveat, we should always take sin seriously and not make excuses for them no matter how valid our reasons may be to us.

Justification of wrongdoing can mean the loss of a blessed state before God. And the practicing of consulting a familiar spirit and divination was a high offense, not only towards God but towards his people, for they were supposed to serve Elohim in righteousness and be a nation to the nations.

Therefore, Saul consulting a medium was a terrible and despicable before God. Saul knew better, and God holds leaders accountable over others who have no knowledge. Those who are ignorant are held to a God's standards as those who are knowledgeable as well but those who are knowledgeable are "beaten with many stripes," and those who are ignorant just a few. Nevertheless, God chastises sin. There are some cases where mercy is given. However, Saul lost the mercy of the Lord because the Lord had turned his back on him. which was a horrible position for him to be in.

> The more Saul pursued David, the more he was bucking against the will of God and trying to exert his own will making himself vile before the Lord and his sin as witchcraft before the Lord, because he was acting in hostile rebellion. "Saul groaned to his armor bearer, "take your sword and Kill me before these pagan philistines come to run me through and taunt and torture me' But his armor bearer was afraid and would not do it. So Saul took his own sword and fell on it" (1st Samuel 31:4).

Chapter 22

Spirit of Death

King Saul's rebellion would lead to his own suicide, a grim and dark way for him to go. As he trespassed against God, he found himself so much in despair that it ended with him falling on his own sword. (Caveat, don't let yourself become so disobedient that you fall on your own sword. A lot of people defeat themselves and that is why they do not make it in life. It's not their upbringing that defeats them or their enemies, but it is their own bad choices that lead to their defeat). Saul would become Israel's disgraced first king. I wonder if he had to fall on his sword?

Sometimes things don't have to end the way they do, but they do. We do it to ourselves. Saul was possessed with a devil and the devil took him out. A person can't serve the devil and have the devil turn on him or her. This is the nature of the beast. Rebellion will always lead to disgrace and misfortune. The lie of Satan is to make you think you can prosper or stay prosperous in sin.

Saul's epithet reads, "Moral Failure." And David's reads, "Heart excellence," because his heart was in line with God. Although there were moments of straying, he always came back to Elohim Saul strayed until eternal damnation and shall be judged when God will bring into account all things. And from the looks at his life through scripture, he will not have a favorable disposition of the Lord.

And this is the lot of all those that reject the Lord and his commands, exalting their will above the will of a holy God who has prescribed his will for his creation to abide in his love and to receive the blessing of keeping His commands and doing things His way. And might I add, His will is based on the virtues of love and not as a God who seeks to promote His authority over one's life, but prescribes His commands to protect us from harm's way.

"And his men and their families all moved to Judah, and they settled in their villages near Hebrom. The men of Judah came to David and anointed him king over the people of Judah" (2 Samuel 2:3-4).

Chapter 23

Claiming New Territory

After every struggle there is new territory that one gains. It is a spiritual reward for the battle fought. The Lord does not hesitate to give us glory of territory. It is the reason why we fought so hard to begin with. Now David knew what he would gain as a king because he was anointed to be king.

However, sometimes, if not most times, the territory we gain is a surprise to us. However, it is utopia once we get there. David was anointed three times to be king. Gaining the tribe of Judah was prophetic, because Jesus would be the lion from that tribe.

There were spiritual blessings attached to gaining that land and there are spiritual blessings attached to gaining our territory as well. We must do our best to keep that territory as well, because we will have a later fight for that territory as Satan never wants us to enjoy that territory given to us by the Lord.

David was anointed a second time, assuring him that he was God's choice. Later on he would gain the territory of Israel and be anointed there as well, now the number 3 is a number for eternity. David would forever be a prototype for all kings to come, and Jesus would always be known to sit on the throne of David, an honor no other man would receive because of his heart and mind as king. May we live for God and may we gain newfound territory eternally on earth and in heaven.

Epilogue

The Echoes of the Timber Wolf is the call to courage to know and understand God on a deeper level. The wolf is symbolic of power, courage, and spirit. Now that you have turned the pages of this book, may the Lord take you and challenge you in strange but blessed ways, and may you learn what it's like to be made by trouble and crowned by joy as David was so many eons ago.

Afterword

This book has been in the making for nearly 25 years, ever since I became a lover of the character of David. I was about 19 when that began. I had been saved and become a Christian when I was 16, while facing a life sentence in prison. It was towards the end of that ordeal that I began to make it my sincere prayer to be a man after God's own heart. I have been praying that prayer daily since.I have read many books, researched him thoroughly, talked with people in the ministry about this very complicated man in the biblical text, and have discovered that David was larger than life and a story that legends are made of, My hope is that this book will thrill you and take you into the mind and heart of God as He chooses us in His providence .

About the author

Jean Belizaire has been in ministry nearly 20 years and is a native of Brockton, Massachusetts He is the former pastor of South Baptist Church in New Bedford Mass. Jean prides himself in being a published author of three previous works; *Rebirth and Revival of a Rebel, The Scorpion and the Chameleon the ending of Voodoo and Black Magic, and Wanganeges, The Power of Women Yesterday, Today, and Forever"*. In his private time Jean enjoys studying history and culture.